BBC Gardeners' World

POCKET PLANTS

CLIMBERS

Andi Clevely

BBC Books

Author Biography
Andi Clevely has been a working gardener for nearly thirty years. He began his career in Leeds City Council central nurseries and since then has worked in many gardens around the country, including Windsor Great Park. He is now responsible for a country estate and large garden in Stratford-on-Avon where he lives with his family. Andi has written a number of gardening books and presents a weekly gardening programme.

Acknowledgements
The publishers would like to thank Busheyfields Climbers Nursery, Herne, Kent; Longstock Park Nursery, Stockbridge, Hampshire; Secretts Garden Centre, Godalming, Surrey, and The Royal Horticultural Society Gardens, Wisley, Surrey, for their assistance with the photography. Photographs by Jo Whitworth © BBC except the following pages: Garden Picture Library 7, 38 (John Glover), 23, 45 (Howard Rice), 30, 54 (Philippe Bonduel), 32 (Neil Holmes), 53 (Brian Carter); Harry Smith Collection 14, 21, 22, 28, 39, 47; Holt Studios 33; John Glover 79; Photos Horticultural 16, 46, 68.

Published by BBC Books, an imprint of BBC Worldwide Limited,
Woodlands, 80 Wood Lane, London W12 0TT

First published 1998
© BBC Worldwide Limited 1998
The moral right of the author has been asserted

ISBN 0 563 38421 2

Artwork by Pond and Giles

Set in Futura

Printed and bound in Belgium by Proost NV
Colour separations by Radstock Reproductions Limited, Midsomer Norton, Avon
Cover printed in Belgium by Proost NV

Choosing a Climber for your Garden

Bold denotes
evergreen

INTRODUCTION

A rich and varied repertoire of versatile climbers, ramblers and wall shrubs is available for growing on garden walls, fences and similar upright structures which offer inviting opportunities to add vertical interest to planting schemes. With imaginative selection plants can be used to soften the angles of buildings, camouflage an eyesore, or turn a garden shed or gateway into a decorative feature.

Planning

Each species has its own unique character, vigour and habit: it might provide strong colour in summer or an interesting evergreen background in winter.

Some climbers complement their surroundings, while others screen or disguise their supports. Existing shrubs could host a gracefully draped rambler.

Vigorous twining species such as vines, wisteria or aristolochia quickly bring plain structures such as archways or arbours to life, and when trained on free-standing trellis can create an effective windbreak. Experiment with growing two or more species together, either for colour contrast or to extend the flowering season. And remember, many climbers deserve prominence as soloists, growing on pillars or trellis pyramids as highlights in flower borders.

Growing conditions

Aspect: A wall or fence can face any direction and so modify the amount of light a plant receives. Check whether your choice needs sun or a certain amount of shade (some plants tolerate either). Occasionally this can be critical: a camellia may not flower well if exposed to early sunlight on a frosty morning.

Shelter: A warm sunny wall or the angle between two fences can provide a sheltered niche in which a slightly tender species can survive the winter, so reserve these sites for plants of borderline hardiness. Wind affects growth, and a fence or screen offers protection for brittle stems and sensitive blooms.

Drainage: The soil at the foot of a wall can be very dry in summer, and it is often important to water plants growing there or add plenty of humus to the soil. But make sure that water does not drain or collect there, compromising drainage and encouraging root diseases that flourish in waterlogged soil.

Preparing the ground

The planting site for perennial species is best prepared in late summer or autumn by digging or forking one or two spits deep over an area at least a metre (yard) square for each plant. Remove all weeds, especially perennial kinds, and then improve the soil according to its type.

Heavy soils: Clay tends to be sticky in winter and hard in summer, so dig in plenty of grit or fine gravel to aerate the soil and improve its drainage. Work in coarse humus such as garden compost or partly rotted leaf mould before planting, and afterwards keep the surface covered with a coarse mulch to stabilize its structure: cocoa shells or shredded bark are ideal materials.

Light soils: Plenty of moisture-retentive material is important to prevent sandy soils from drying out quickly. Garden compost, leaf mould, well-rotted manure and composted bark are all suitable, reinforced by a slow-release fertilizer such as bonemeal as nutrients leach quickly from light soils. Mulching will also help to keep roots moist.

Planting

Plants bought in pots may be planted whenever the soil is not too wet or frozen, although autumn or spring are best; these times are especially important for bare-rooted plants. Optimum seasons are given in the individual entries.

The same simple planting procedure applies to most species.

- Prepare the site thoroughly beforehand, preferably several weeks earlier.

- Position the plant carefully on the surface; do not plant it right next to a wall where the soil will be driest, but leave a distance of at least 30cm (12in). Plant about 1.8m (6ft) away from trees to avoid competition for water.

- Dig out a hole large enough to accommodate the roots comfortably, and at the same depth as the plant was previously growing.

- Break up the excavated soil, backfill around the plant and firm gently into place. Water in well if planting in dry weather, and mulch where recommended.

- Make sure supports are in position beforehand. Insert canes near the base of the plant, especially where initial guidance is suggested in the text, and tie the stems in place pointing towards their main support.

Support

A few natural scramblers may be left to their own devices if they are self-clinging or growing next to suitable host plants, but most will need artificial support of some kind. This can be a few wall nails inserted in mortar joints for securing woody branches, a simple cane to lead young stems into a tree where they will then be self-supporting, or some twiggy peasticks for slender annual growth.

Most other plants need a more permanent arrangement. Panels of wooden trellis are effective; taut wires (vertical or horizontal) or sections of wide-mesh wire netting, attached to vine eyes to keep them a short distance from the wall, are strong and unobtrusive. Make sure all main supports are sturdy and secure, and regularly treated with preservative if needed.

Care

Watering: Regular watering is important until new plants are established and growing strongly, especially in a hot summer or when they are growing against a dry wall.

Always soak plants, but guard against waterlogging. Mature plants seldom need much water, particularly if they are mulched over the root area.

Feeding: Some species derive adequate nourishment from an annual mulch, while others need one or more dressings of fertilizer each season specific requirements are given in the entries. Slow-release mixtures are best for spring application and will last all year; during the growing season use fast-acting liquid feeds to sustain growth.

Pruning: Specific details are given in the entries. Most young plants need formative pruning to concentrate growth into a few strong well-placed stems that will establish the final shape of the plant. After this, maintenance pruning aims to direct growth wherever it is required, limit the plant's size to the available space and renew flowering stems where appropriate. Always cut out dead and diseased wood first, before starting to prune sound stems.

Abelia × grandiflora Abelia

ABELIA × GRANDIFLORA 'FRANCIS MASON'

This is a vigorous climber, with a long season of lightly fragrant blooms that continue well into autumn, when they are a popular food source for late bees. It is ideal for a warm wall, especially near the sea, or as camouflage at the base of a bare-stemmed climber.

Habit:	Hardy or slightly tender perennial wall shrub; vigorous but brittle arching stems.
Flowering time:	Mid-summer to mid-autumn.
Foliage:	Glossy, light green or variegated; semi-evergreen in mild areas.
Size:	1.5m (5ft) high; 1.5–1.8m (5–6ft) wide.
Positioning:	Full sun or light shade, sheltered from winds; in well-drained soil.
Care:	Plant in spring in well-dug soil with added compost and feed with general fertilizer. Mulch in autumn with compost or leaf mould. In cold gardens cut down growth first, or grow in pots and over-winter indoors. Train stems on trellis or wires. In spring cut back dead shoots, thin dense twiggy growth.
Propagation:	Grow cuttings under glass in summer, in a frame in autumn.
Recommended:	Basic hybrid; 'Francis Mason' (variegated).
Useful tip:	Variegated forms colour best in full sun and dry soils.

Akebia quinata Chocolate Vine

Habit: Hardy perennial climber; with vigorous twining woody stems.

Flowering time: Late spring and early summer.

Foliage: Divided into 3–5 oval leaflets, sometimes sparse; deep blue-green; deciduous or semi-evergreen.

Size: 10m (33ft) or more high; 1.8m (6ft) wide.

Positioning: Sun or shade, on a high wall or tall tree, as a screen; in any fairly fertile soil.

Care: Plant in autumn or spring in well-dug soil with a little added humus. In spring feed with general fertilizer, mulch on light soils. Train on wires or trellis, or on canes into the branches of a tree. Trim plants to size if necessary in autumn.

Propagation: Grow cuttings under glass in summer; layer in winter.

Recommended: Basic species only; also A. *trifoliata*, with larger fruit.

Useful tip: This is one of the best climbers to grow on a totally shaded wall, or as a background to flowering plants.

AKEBIA QUINATA

This vigorous ornamental climber can tolerate full shade and is an excellent choice for disguising a shed or unwelcome eyesore. It is grown mainly for its foliage: a good display of the spicily fragrant blooms depends on a mild spring, while the deep purple fruits, up to 10cm (4in) long, require a long hot summer.

Ampelopsis heterophylla Ampelopsis

AMPELOPSIS HETEROPHYLLA 'ELEGANS'

This robust vine can be relied on to cover a large pergola, shed or screen, and will also scramble gracefully from high trees. The more restrained 'Elegans' has pretty pink, cream and yellow markings. Both bear bunches of porcelain-blue 'grapes' after a hot summer. (syn. *A. glandulosa* var. *brevipedunculata*.)

Habit:	Hardy perennial climber; woody stems and curling self-supporting tendrils.
Flowering time:	Late summer.
Foliage:	Heart-shaped or divided into leaflets; dark green or variegated; deciduous.
Size:	5m (16ft) or more high; 3m (10ft) wide.
Positioning:	Full sun or very light shade, on strong supports; in any soil. Grow on a sunny site for fruits.
Care:	Plant in autumn or spring in well-dug soil with a little added compost or bonemeal. Feed in spring with half-strength general fertilizer, and mulch. Train young stems on wires or trellis until self-supporting. Trim to size in late winter.
Propagation:	Grow cuttings in a frame in mid-summer.
Recommended:	Basic species and variegated 'Elegans' (syn. 'Tricolor'); also *A. megalophylla*.
Useful tip:	Grow variegated forms in light shade to prevent hot sunshine scorching the leaves.

Aristolochia durior
Dutchman's Pipe, Birthwort

Habit: Hardy or slightly tender perennial climber; very vigorous twining stems.

Flowering time: Late spring to mid-summer.

Foliage: Large, heart-shaped and prolific, matt green; deciduous.

Size: Up to 9m (30ft) high; 6m (20ft) wide.

Positioning: Full sun or very light shade, sheltered from cold winds, on strong supports; in moist leafy soil.

Care: Plant in spring in well dug soil with plenty of compost or leaf mould and feed with general fertilizer. Mulch in autumn, especially on cold soils. Support stems with netting or trellis on bare walls. Thin overgrown stems in spring.

Propagation: Grow cuttings under glass in summer; divide roots in spring.

Recommended: Basic species only.

Useful tip: Other popular species, such as A. littoralis and A. sempervirens should not be attempted outdoors, but make vigorous and exotic climbers for a heated conservatory wall.

ARISTOLOCHIA DURIOR

Very few Aristolochia species are hardy, and even this one may be cut down to ground level by frost In exceptionally cold winters. It will recover quickly, though, to cover a summerhouse, pillar or arbour with its dense exotic foliage and curious siphon-shaped blooms. (syns A. macrophylla, A. sipho.)

Asteranthera ovata Asteranthera

ASTERANTHERA OVATA

The temperate forests of Chile are home to this fascinating creeper, so it is most likely to be successful when given the moist shade and leafy soil of its native habitat – try growing it against a damp wall or over a tree stump. Plants are hardy only to –5°C (23°F), but cuttings are easy and should be taken each year as an insurance. (syn. *Columnea ovata*.)

Habit:	Hardy or slightly tender perennial creeper; aerial roots trail or scramble.
Flowering time:	Early to late summer.
Foliage:	Small, rounded or rectangular, toothed; dark green; more or less evergreen.
Size:	3–4m (10–13ft) high; up to 3m (10ft) wide.
Positioning:	Semi-shade with shelter from cold winds and frost, among shrubs or on walls and fences; in moist leafy soil without too much lime.
Care:	Plant in spring in well-dug soil with plenty of compost or leaf mould and feed with general fertilizer. Mulch in spring and autumn; water regularly in a dry season, but let the compost surface dry out between waterings. Allow to grow freely. Pruning is unnecessary.
Propagation:	Grow cuttings in a frame in summer; layer in autumn.
Recommended:	Basic species only.
Useful tip:	Stems root freely at leaf joints and may be left to spread as ground cover beneath shrubs.

Berberidopsis corallina Coral Plant

Habit: Hardy or slightly tender perennial climber; scrambling or twining woody stems.

Flowering time: Early summer to early autumn.

Foliage: Oval or heart-shaped; leathery and edged with small spines; evergreen

Size: 3–4m (10–13ft) high; up to 3m (10ft) wide.

Positioning: Light or semi-shade, with shelter from cold winds, on walls and shrubs; in moist fertile lime-free soil.

Care: Plant in spring in well-dug soil with plenty of compost or leaf mould and feed with general fertilizer. Mulch lavishly in spring and autumn. Support with wires or trellis on walls, or train into shrubs. Trim excess growth in spring or autumn.

Propagation: Grow cuttings under glass in mid-summer or layer in autumn.

Recommended: Basic species only.

Useful tip: Provided the roots are mulched in autumn, plants injured by frost will re-sprout from the base in spring.

BERBERIDOPSIS CORALLINA

Shade and shelter are essential for this beautiful evergreen climber, so plant it among shrubs and trees, especially any that will support its rambling stems and keep cold winds at bay. The hanging clusters of blooms gleam like jewels against the contrasting grey-green foliage.

Bignonia capreolata Trumpet Flower, Cross Vine

BIGNONIA CAPREOLATA

The growth of this North American vine can be rampant on a sunny sheltered wall, where the evergreen or semi-evergreen foliage provides a dense foil for the eye-catching summer display of 5cm (2in) funnel-shaped flowers. A warm position is essential. (syn. *Doxantha capreolata*.)

Habit: Hardy or slightly tender perennial climber; self-supporting with leaf tendrils.

Flowering time: Early and mid-summer.

Foliage: Long, divided into 2 narrow leaflets; more or less evergreen.

Size: 9m (30ft) or more high; 4m (13ft) wide.

Positioning: Full sun, protected by a warm wall or fence; in rich well-drained soil.

Care: Plant in spring in deeply dug soil with plenty of compost or well-rotted manure and feed with general fertilizer. In mild gardens restrain roots with slates. Mulch in spring and autumn with compost or leaf mould. Spread out the young stems to encourage wide coverage. Prune in spring only if needed, shortening the main stems by one-third.

Propagation: Grow cuttings under glass in late summer; layer in autumn.

Recommended: Basic species only.

Useful tip: A superb species for training into a large tree or sunny hedge in mild gardens.

Billardiera longiflora Blueberry

Habit: Hardy or slightly tender perennial climber; slender twining woody stems.

Flowering time: Early to late summer.

Foliage: Narrow and lance-shaped; evergreen.

Size: 1.8m (6ft) high; 1.2–1.5m (4–5ft) wide.

Positioning: Full sun, under cold glass or on a warm wall sheltered from cold winds; in rich lime-free soil.

Care: Plant in spring in well-dug soil with plenty of compost or leaf mould and feed with rhododendron fertilizer. Mulch in spring and autumn. Support with wires or trellis on a wall or fence, train through a wall shrub. Cut out weak and dead shoots in mid-spring.

Propagation: Grow cuttings under glass in summer; sow seeds under glass in spring.

Recommended: Basic species; also 'Rosea' (pink fruits).

Useful tip: In cold gardens, grow on a trellis in large containers and bring indoors for winter.

BILLARDIERA LONGIFLORA

Demurely attractive in summer when laden with small greenish-yellow bells, this Australian evergreen, with its rich green foliage, becomes a real highlight in the autumn. As the heavy crops of 2.5cm (1in) berries mature, they often vary in colour between blue, purple and red on the same vine. Plants are only just hardy and benefit from frost-protection in cold gardens.

Bomarea caldasii Bomarea

BOMAREA CALDASII

This handsome species is only marginally hardy and normally needs a sheltered position or prime site in a cold conservatory if winters tend to be very cold. The tuberous roots run deep, however, and can often survive outdoors under a thick winter blanket of straw. (syn. *B. kalbreyeri*.)

Habit: Slightly tender tuberous-rooted perennial climber; twining herbaceous stems.

Flowering time: Late spring to mid-summer.

Foliage: Smooth and broadly lance-shaped, twists to reveal underside; deciduous.

Size: 3–4m (10–13ft) high; up to 1.8m (6ft) wide.

Positioning: Full sun, on a warm frost-free wall or under cold glass; in light fertile soil.

Care: Plant in spring in well-dug soil with added compost (lighten clay soils with grit or coarse sand), feed with general fertilizer and mulch. Water freely while growing. Cut down in autumn when leaves fall and protect roots with a lavish mulch of straw, bracken or leaves.

Propagation: Divide roots in spring.

Recommended: Basic species only; also *B. edulis* (purple-spotted pink flowers).

Useful tip: Grow outdoors on canes in deep pots in summer; overwinter in a frost-free place.

Buddleja alternifolia
Buddleia, Butterfly Bush

Habit:	Hardy perennial wall shrub; densely furnished with slender arching branches.
Flowering time:	Early to mid-summer.
Foliage:	Long, narrow and plentiful; dark grey-green; deciduous.
Size:	4m (13ft) or more high; 4m (13ft) wide.
Positioning:	Full sun or very light shade, on walls and fences; in any soil.
Care:	Plant in autumn or spring in well-dug soil with added compost and bonemeal. Feed in spring with general fertilizer. Tie in new stems on wires or trellis as they develop. Prune immediately after flowering: remove about one-third of oldest stems from as low down as required.
Propagation:	Grow cuttings in a frame in autumn.
Recommended:	Basic species and silvery-leated 'Argentea'; also *B. fallowiana* and its white form var. *alba*, and similar 'Lochinch'.
Useful tip:	May also be trained from a high bed or container to cascade down a wall.

BUDDLEJA ALTERNIFOLIA

This elegant species is early flowering on last year's stems, unlike other buddleias, and has leaves arranged alternately along its slim branches, which bend gracefully under the weight of foliage and flowers. It is easily trained as a fan with the ends of branches allowed to arch forwards as they come into bloom.

CAMELLIA JAPONICA

Although perfectly hardy, camellias enjoy warmth and protection, together with a little shade from early sunshine which can spoil the buds and blooms. A well-grown flowering specimen looks magnificent, whether it is allowed to grow informally or trained symmetrically as a fan or espalier, in the way that a fruit tree is trained against a wall.

Habit: Hardy perennial wall shrub; slow-growing woody stems.

Flowering time: Late winter to mid-spring.

Foliage: Glossy, pointed with serrated edges; evergreen.

Size: Up to 3m (10ft) high; 1.8–3m (6–10ft) wide.

Positioning: Full sun or light shade, sheltered from cold winds and early morning sunshine, on walls and fences; in well-drained acid soil.

Care: Plant in spring in deeply dug soil with added compost or leaf mould, feed with rhododendron fertilizer and mulch. Train stems on wires or trellis. Deadhead if necessary. Prune after flowering: shorten unwanted stems to 2–3 buds.

Propagation: Layer in early spring.

Recommended: C. × williamsii 'Anticipation', 'Donation', 'Leonard Messel'; C. japonica 'Hagoromo', 'Nobilissima'.

Useful tip: Water regularly with rainwater when dry.

Campsis radicans Trumpet Creeper

Habit: Hardy perennial climber; strong woody stems, aerial roots.

Flowering time: Late summer until autumn frosts.

Foliage: Divided into numerous leaflets; dark green, downy; deciduous.

Size: Up to 9m (30ft) high; 3m (10ft) or more wide.

Positioning: Full sun, some shelter from cold winds; moist but well-drained soil.

Care: Plant in spring in deeply dug soil with plenty of compost or well-rotted manure, feed with general fertilizer, mulch light soils. Train stems on wires or trellis until self-supporting. In winter thin congested stems and shorten others to 2–3 buds.

Propagation: Grow cuttings in a frame in summer, layer in winter.

Recommended: Basic species and *flava* (syn. 'Yellow Trumpet'); also *C. × tagliabuana* 'Madame Galen' (less hardy).

Useful tip: To train formally like a grape vine, prune side-shoots back to short spurs.

CAMPSIS RADICANS

This is a native of the United States and a close relative of the trumpet flower (*Bignonia*). It is an agile creeper, capable of smothering an old tree, outhouse or high wall with a glorious display of brilliant trumpet-shaped blooms, up to 8cm (3in) long, set against a solid backdrop of attractive foliage.

17

CARPENTERIA CALIFORNICA

This lovely Californian shrub deserves a prominent place in any garden with a sheltered site at the foot of a sunny wall, even though it is not always long-lived. Plants are normally hardy down to −5°C (23°F), but the large-flowered selection 'Bodnant', with blooms 8cm (3in) or more across, is tougher and a good choice for cold districts.

Habit:	Hardy or slightly tender perennial wall shrub; lax sprawling stems.
Flowering time:	Mid- and late summer.
Foliage:	Narrowly oval or oblong; glossy dark green; evergreen.
Size:	1.5–1.8m (5–6ft) high; up to 1.8m (6ft) wide.
Positioning:	Full sun or light shade, on walls or fences sheltered from cold winds; in any well-drained soil.
Care:	Plant in spring in well-dug soil with a little added garden compost and bonemeal, feed with general fertilizer and mulch on light soils. Allow to grow informally or train stems as a fan on wires or trellis. Prune to shape after flowering.
Propagation:	Grow cuttings under glass in summer.
Recommended:	Basic species and larger-flowered forms 'Bodnant' and 'Ladham's Variety'.
Useful tip:	Choose plants while in bloom, as some are seed-raised and variable in quality.

Ceanothus (deciduous) Californian Lilac

Habit:	Hardy perennial wall shrub; vigorous branching stems.
Flowering time:	Mid-summer to mid-autumn.
Foliage:	Soft and broadly pointed; mid-green; deciduous.
Size:	1.5–1.8m (5–6ft) high; up to 1.8m (6ft) wide.
Positioning:	Full sun, with a little shelter from cold winds, on pergolas, arbours and walls; in poor well-drained soil.
Care:	Plant in spring in well-broken soil with added bonemeal; open heavy soils with dressings of grit. Feed in spring with half-strength general fertilizer. Tie main branches to wires or nails. After flowering shorten side-shoots to 2–3 buds beyond their base.
Propagation:	Grow cuttings in a frame in autumn.
Recommended:	C. × delileanus 'Gloire de Versailles', less hardy 'Topaz'; also C. × pallidus 'Marie Simon', 'Perle Rose'.
Useful tip:	Overgrown plants may be cut back hard in late winter.

CEANOTHUS 'GLOIRE DE VERSAILLES'

There are fewer deciduous Ceanothus than evergreen kinds, but they tend to be tidier and less particular about aspect and soil conditions. They grow fast and quickly develop into satisfyingly rounded shrubs. They may also be wall-trained as handsome backing for late-flowering lilies and other flowers.

Ceanothus (evergreen) California Lilac

CEANOTHUS 'BLUE CUSHION'

Evergreen Ceanothus varieties are popular choices for growing against walls, partly because they appreciate the warmth and shelter there, and also because they make an attractive background all the year round. Varieties with smaller leaves are often the hardiest.

Habit: Hardy or slightly tender perennial wall shrub; stiff bushy stems.

Flowering time: Late spring, summer or early autumn according to variety.

Foliage: Oval, sometimes very small; glossy bright green; evergreen.

Size: Up to 3m (10ft) high; 3–4m (10–13ft) wide.

Positioning: Full sun, with shelter from cold winds, on walls and fences; in poor well-drained soil without too much lime.

Care: Plant in spring in well-broken soil with added bonemeal; work plenty of grit into heavy soils. Tie in main branches to wires or wall nails. Trim after flowering, starting while plants are still young; avoid cutting into old wood.

Propagation: Grow cuttings in a frame in summer.

Recommended: Hardiest: 'Concha', 'Delight', 'Autumnal Blue', 'Puget Blue', 'Burkwoodii'. Slightly tender: 'Italian Skies', 'Trewithen Blue'.

Useful tip: Neglected or top-heavy bushes are best replaced from cuttings.

Celastrus orbiculatus Staff Vine, Oriental Bittersweet

Habit: Hardy perennial climber; vigorous and densely tangled twining stems.

Flowering time: Summer (insignificant).

Foliage: Rounded; pale green turning yellow in autumn; deciduous.

Size: Up to 12m (40ft) high; 3m (10ft) wide.

Positioning: Full sun or light shade, with strong support like a full-size tree; in any soil.

Care: Plant in autumn or spring in well-dug soil with a little added compost. Feeding is unnecessary, but mulch light soils in spring. Train stems into a tree or on wires against a high wall or fence. Prune in late winter if necessary: cut out weak and invasive shoots.

Propagation: Layer in summer; grow cuttings outdoors in autumn.

Recommended: Basic species (hermaphrodite form); also *C. scandens*, similar, less vigorous.

Useful tip: Seeds may be overwintered in dry sand in a frame and sown in spring.

CELASTRUS ORBICULATUS

This energetic climber needs plenty of room and a position where its spectacular autumn display of colour can be enjoyed fully. At the same time as the shapely leaves turn clear yellow, the brownish-orange seed capsules split to expose scarlet seeds that defy birds and often last all winter.

Chaenomeles speciosa Flowering Quince

CHAENOMELES SPECIOSA VAR.

This popular shrub is easily grown and is especially attractive when trained formally against a house wall or fence. The extra pruning this involves produces masses of short neat spurs that are smothered for six weeks or more with spring blossom, which is often followed in late summer by apple- or pear-shaped fruits.

Habit:	Hardy perennial wall shrub; strong upright thorny branches.
Flowering time:	Early to mid-spring.
Foliage:	Small, shiny and oval; appears after flowers; deciduous.
Size:	Up to 3m (10ft) high; 2.4m (8ft) wide.
Positioning:	Full sun or semi-shade; in any soil. Tolerates draughts and exposure.
Care:	Plant in autumn or spring in well-dug soil with added compost or bonemeal. Feed in spring with general fertilizer. Mulch in autumn. Train stems evenly on wires or trellis. Cut back side-shoots in summer to 2–3 leaves; trim in spring to just beyond the flower buds.
Propagation:	Grow cuttings under glass in summer; layer in autumn.
Recommended:	Many good forms include 'Geisha Girl', 'Apple Blossom' (syn. 'Moerloosii'), 'Nivalis' and 'Simonii'.
Useful tip:	*C. × superba* varieties are less upright and produce wide sprawling bushes.

Chimonanthus praecox Wintersweet

Habit: Hardy perennial wall shrub; slender branching stems.

Flowering time: Early to late winter.

Foliage: Oval and rough; matt green; deciduous.

Size: 2.4m (8ft) or more high; 3m (10ft) wide.

Positioning: Full sun, with shelter from cold winds, on a warm wall; in deep fertile soil (not acid).

Care: Plant in autumn or spring in deeply dug soil with plenty of well rotted manure or compost and bonemeal. Feed in spring with general fertilizer, and mulch light soils. Train branches horizontally or as a fan on wires. After flowering, cut all side-shoots to 1–2 buds from their base.

Propagation: Layer stems in spring or summer.

Recommended: Basic species and larger-flowered forms 'Grandiflorus' and 'Luteus'.

Useful tip: Plants may look dull after flowering, so combine them with a clematis such as C. alpina for extended colour.

CHIMONANTHUS PRAECOX

It may be several years after planting before the leafless branches are studded with their fragrant waxy flowers, but the delay is worthwhile. The basic species has the sweetest perfume, and a cut branch brought indoors can scent a whole room for days on end. Firm pruning ensures plenty of blossom each winter.
(syn. *C. fragrans*.)

Clematis armandii Armand's Clematis

CLEMATIS ARMANDII

The earliest of the spring-flowering clematis, this evergreen species needs plenty of space, ideally on a warm wall or in a large sheltered tree where it can show off its delicately coloured single blooms with their vanilla fragrance. Try cutting long flowering strands for indoor decoration.

Habit: Hardy or slightly tender perennial climber; vigorous flexible stems and twining leaf stalks.

Flowering time: Mid- to late spring.

Foliage: Glossy, dark and leathery; divided into 3 leaflets; evergreen.

Size: 3–5m (10–16ft) high; 1.8–3m (6–10ft) wide.

Positioning: Full sun or very light shade, sheltered from cold winds and severe frost; in rich well-drained soil.

Care: Plant in autumn or spring in deeply dug soil with plenty of compost. Mulch in spring; water regularly in a dry season. Tie young stems to wires or trellis; they will then be self-supporting. Prune, if needed, after flowering: cut side-shoots above a leaf joint near their base.

Propagation: Layer, or grow cuttings under glass in summer.

Recommended: Basic species; also pink 'Apple Blossom' and white 'Snowdrift'.

Useful tip: Failing a warm sheltered wall, grow this in a conservatory or in a sunny porch for protection.

Clematis (late) Clematis

Habit: Hardy perennial climber; rampant scrambling self-supporting stems.

Flowering time: Mid- or late summer to late autumn.

Foliage: Divided into 5 leaflets; mid-green; deciduous.

Size: 4m (13ft) high; 1.8m (6ft) or more wide.

Positioning: Full sun, in warmth on a wall or tree stump; in free-draining soil.

Care: Plant in autumn or spring in deeply dug soil with some compost. Mulch in spring. Train stems horizontally on wires or evenly over a free-standing support. In late winter or early spring cut stems back to about 30cm (12in) above ground level.

Propagation: Layer, or grow cuttings under glass in summer.

Recommended: Other late varieties include 'Lady Betty Balfour', 'Duchess of Albany' and 'Ernest Markham'.

Useful tip: The flowers are sterile and therefore last longer than usual, especially in flower arrangements.

CLEMATIS VITICELLA PURPUREA PLENA 'ELEGANS'

Clematis varieties that continue flowering until the autumn frosts are always welcome climbers. This is one of the latest and most vigorous free-flowering varieties, with fully double rosettes that look spectacular on plants that are allowed to scramble over low walls, a tree stump or a large shrub.

Clematis (mid-season) Clematis

CLEMATIS 'VICTORIA'

'Victoria' is a classic large-flowered Jackmanii variety of clematis, whose 15cm (6in) blooms are so numerous that they will cover a large area of wall for several weeks. It is one of the best kinds for massed impact, and also for planting as a companion with a strong climbing rose.

Habit: Hardy perennial climber; very strong vigorous self-supporting stems.

Flowering time: Early summer to early autumn.

Foliage: Bright, mid-green; very large; deciduous.

Size: 2.4–3m (8–10ft) high; 1.8m (6ft) wide.

Positioning: Sun or shade, on a wall or pergola; in rich well-drained soil.

Care: Plant in autumn or spring, 10cm (4in) deeper than the top of the rootball, in deeply dug soil with added compost. Mulch in spring with well-rotted manure. Feed at mid-summer with general fertilizer. Cut growth down in late winter to just above the base of last year's growth.

Propagation: Layer, or grow cuttings under glass in summer.

Recommended: Other mid-season varieties include 'Niobe', 'Marie Boisselot', 'Hagley Hybrid', 'Sunset'.

Useful tip: Train stems in on taller walls and prune very lightly after flowering.

Clematis (species) Clematis

Habit: Hardy perennial climber; vigorous wiry self-supporting stems.

Flowering time: Mid-summer to early autumn.

Foliage: Slender, prettily divided; light green; deciduous.

Size: 4.5–7.5m (15–25ft) high; up to 3m (10ft) wide.

Positioning: Sun or shade, with shelter from cold winds, on walls, large buildings and trees; in very well drained soil.

Care: Plant in autumn or spring in well-dug soil; work plenty of grit or similar coarse material into heavy soils. Mulch in spring; use well-rotted manure on poor soils. Train stems on wires, trellis or netting. In winter cut stems to just above the base of last year's growth.

Propagation: Layer, or grow cuttings under glass in summer.

Recommended: Other fine species include C. *flammula*, C. *macropetala* and C. *rehderiana*.

Useful tip: Cut a few stems of older plants to ground level to renew vigour.

CLEMATIS CAMPANIFLORA

Every clematis has its ideal position, and this *viticella* relative is perfectly suited to an open tree or large shed, which it will drape densely with elegant foliage and small nodding blooms. These sometimes appear to be completely white, and often glisten in the sun with a frosted sheen.

CLIANTHUS PUNICEUS

This sun-loving New Zealand shrub is tall and vigorous and obviously a member of the pea family. It is elegant but unexceptional until its drooping clusters of vivid red blooms, variously compared to parrots or claws, appear. (syns C. 'Red Admiral', 'Red Cardinal'.)

Habit: Slightly tender perennial wall shrub; woody scrambling stems.

Flowering time: Late spring to mid-summer.

Foliage: Numerous leaflets; shiny mid-green; more or less evergreen.

Size: 3m (10ft) or more high; 1.8m (6ft) wide.

Positioning: Full sun, on a warm sheltered wall or in a cool conservatory; in light well-drained soil.

Care: Plant in spring in well-broken soil with added grit (if heavy) or compost (if light) and feed with high-nitrogen fertilizer. In cold areas cover the roots with straw or bracken in autumn, and protect trained stems with sacking. Train stems on netting. Trim to shape after flowering.

Propagation: Grow cuttings under glass in mid-summer.

Recommended: Basic species; also 'Roseus' (syn. 'Flamingo') and 'Albus' (syn. 'White Heron').

Useful tip: The basic species is easily raised from seeds sown indoors in spring.

Cobaea scandens
Cup & Saucer Vine, Cathedral Bells

Habit: Tender perennial climber (often grown as an annual); woody stems, twining tendrils.

Flowering time: Mid-summer to autumn frosts.

Foliage: Divided into 4–6 oval leaflets; fresh green; evergreen in frost-free conditions.

Size: 4–5m (13–16ft) high; 3m (10ft) wide.

Positioning: Full sun, sheltered from cold winds; in poor soil outdoors in mild areas, elsewhere in pots under glass.

Care: Sow seeds under glass in early spring and move on into large pots, or plant out after the last frosts in light soil with a little added compost. Water freely in dry weather. Train on wires or trellis. In spring trim permanent plants to shape.

Propagation: Sow seeds in spring; grow cuttings under glass in summer.

Recommended: Basic species and *alba* (syn. *flore albo*).

Useful tip: Grow in large pots outdoors; cut back top growth in autumn and overwinter the pots under frost-free glass.

COBAEA SCANDENS ALBA

This rampant Central American climber is an excellent subject for a pergola, which it will soon cover with lush foliage and large fragrant bell-shaped flowers, green at first but finally purple or, less commonly, creamy white. It is reliably perennial when grown at 7°C (45°F).

CODONOPSIS CONVOLVULACEA

A native of high Himalayan slopes, this charming species has soft herbaceous growth and surprisingly large blooms that start life as bells but finally open out flat, when they can reach 5cm (2in) across. A fine scrambler to plant beside a conifer or broad-leafed evergreen shrub.

Habit: Hardy perennial climber; slender twining stems.

Flowering time: Early to late summer.

Foliage: Oval or lance-shaped; soft and bright green; deciduous.

Size: Up to 3m (10ft) high; 1.2m (4ft) wide.

Positioning: Dappled sunlight or light shade, scrambling through a tall shrub; in well-drained soil with plenty of humus.

Care: Plant in autumn or spring in deeply dug soil with added compost or leaf mould. Feed in spring with general fertilizer and mulch on light soils. Water now and then in dry weather. Train on trellis or allow to grow through branches. Cut down top growth in late autumn.

Propagation: Sow seeds under glass in spring; grow cuttings in a frame in autumn.

Recommended: Basic species and white form 'Alba'; also *C. viridiflora*.

Useful tip: Roots in shade and top growth in sunlight give the best results.

Coronilla valentina ssp. glauca Crown Vetch

Habit: Hardy or slightly tender perennial wall shrub; dense bushy stems, blue-green when young.

Flowering time: Mid-spring to early summer, then intermittently.

Foliage: Blue-green; divided into 4–6 leaflets; more or less evergreen.

Size: Up to 1.5m (5ft) high on a wall; 90cm (3ft) wide.

Positioning: Full sun, against a fence or wall; in well-drained soil.

Care: Plant in spring in well dug soil, with added grit in heavier ground, compost in light soil, and feed with general fertilizer; mulch sandy soils. Allow to grow informally or tie main stems to trellis. In late winter cut back a few old branches.

Propagation: Grow cuttings in a frame in summer.

Recommended: Basic subspecies; also paler 'Citrina' and less hardy 'Variegata' (creamy white markings).

Useful tip: To revive flowering, cut plants almost to ground level in spring.

CORONILLA VALENTINA SSP. GLAUCA

The pea-like blooms of this bright free-flowering shrub have a fragrance that is sometimes compared to that of peaches, and in a choice position they will continue to appear until the autumn frosts. It survives the winter best at the foot of a warm wall, where a little pruning and training will induce it to double its compact size.

Cytisus battandieri
Pineapple Broom, Moroccan Broom

CYTISUS BATTANDIERI

The elegant silvery foliage of this native Moroccan broom is an attractive background for its dense heads of bright, pineapple-scented pea flowers. Cold winds can injure it when it is grown in the open, but on light soils with the protection of a warm wall it will thrive happily and always excite admiration for its beauty.

Habit: Hardy or slightly tender perennial wall shrub or small tree; lax woody branches.

Flowering time: Early and mid-summer.

Foliage: Divided into 3 leaflets; downy, grey-green; semi-evergreen.

Size: 4–5m (13–16ft) high; 4m (13ft) wide.

Positioning: Full sun, against a warm wall or hedge for maximum flowering; in well-drained poorish soil.

Care: Plant in autumn (light soils) or spring in well-broken soil; add grit if necessary to aid drainage. Fertility is best kept low, so do not feed or mulch. Tie in branches here and there to resist winds. Either avoid pruning, or tidy after flowering without cutting into old wood.

Propagation: Sow pre-soaked seeds in a frame in spring.

Recommended: Basic species and selected form 'Yellow Tail'.

Useful tip: On chalky soils make sure bought plants are grafted as seedlings dislike lime.

34

Habit: Hardy or slightly tender perennial climber; slender flexible stems and leaf tendrils.

Flowering time: Early summer until autumn frosts.

Foliage: Small; numerous heart-shaped leaflets; mid-green; deciduous.

Size: Up to 3m (10ft) high; 90cm (3ft) wide.

Positioning: Full sun, sheltered from winds, beside a tall hedge or bush; in fertile free-draining soil.

Care: Plant after the last frosts, in groups of 3, in well-dug soil with added compost or leaf mould. Water well initially in dry weather. Train stems on wires or let them scramble through plants. In cold gardens protect roots with straw or leaves in autumn. Cut out dead shoots in spring.

Propagation: Sow seeds under glass in spring.

Recommended: Basic species; also *aurantiacus, roseus* and *coccineus*.

Useful tip: Gather some of the lavish crops of seeds each year as an insurance against winter losses.

ECCREMOCARPUS SCABER

This South American perennial is often grown as a half-hardy annual, but in a warm sheltered position it will survive for many years, even if cut to the ground by frost. Plants need a host shrub or hedge to scramble through and decorate with their cones of vivid blooms.

Euonymus fortunei Dwarf Spindle

Habit: Hardy perennial wall shrub; bushy upright branches and aerial roots as a climber.

Flowering time: Late spring (insignificant).

Foliage: Oval or elliptical; bright green or variegated; evergreen.

Size: Up to 6m (20ft) high on a wall; 3m (10ft) wide.

Positioning: Full sun or very light shade (coloured forms), or semi-shade (green forms), on a wall or fence; in fertile well-drained soil.

Care: Plant in autumn or spring, singly or 23cm (9in) apart for rapid coverage, in well-broken soil with a little bonemeal. In spring apply half-strength general fertilizer. Cut back growth by one-third after planting and train in to wires. Trim to shape in spring.

Propagation: Grow cuttings under glass in summer or in a frame in winter.

Recommended: 'Coloratus', 'Emerald 'n' Gold', 'Variegatus' (syn. 'Silver Gem').

Useful tip: Plants tolerate sea spray, urban pollution.

EUONYMUS FORTUNEI 'EMERALD 'N' GOLD'

Few shrubs are tougher or more obliging than the evergreen dwarf spindles. Grown against a wall, they change from restrained shrubs into ambitious climbers that can eventually reach the eaves of a house. Plants are indifferent to aspect – although variegated forms colour more brightly in the sun – and dry soil does not inhibit their growth.

Fallopia baldschuanica Russian Vine, Mile-a-Minute Vine

Habit: Hardy perennial climber; rampant woody twining stems.

Flowering time: Mid-summer until autumn frosts.

Foliage: Heart- or arrow-shaped, up to 10cm (4in) long; light green; deciduous.

Size: Up to 12m (40ft) high; 6m (20ft) or more wide.

Positioning: Full sun or semi-shade, on a large strong support (not suitable for walls); in any well-drained soil.

Care: Plant in autumn or spring in well-broken soil with a little added bonemeal. Feeding in later life encourages foliage at the expense of flowers. Train stems initially on canes or wires. Prune after flowering or in late winter: remove excess growth and tie in wayward shoots.

Propagation: Grow cuttings under glass in summer or in a frame in autumn.

Recommended: Basic species only.

Useful tip: Although perfectly happy in shade, plants flower best in full sun.

FALLOPIA BALDSCHUANICA

This is the ultimate screening plant. Growth can extend by as much as 5m (16ft) each season, so plan carefully before choosing this enthusiastic Iranian climber which smothers anything in its path. (syn. *Polygonum baldschuanicum*.)

Ficus pumila
Creeping fig

FICUS PUMILA

Although reliably hardy only to −5°C (23°F), outdoor plants often survive happily on warm shady walls, where they can reach a remarkable height. At the top of their self-clinging stems the leaves change into a larger, more mature form. Plants rarely fruit in a cool climate. (syns *F. repens*, *F. stipulata*.)

Habit:	Slightly tender perennial climber; aerial roots.
Flowering time:	Rarely occurs (flowers invisible inside fruits).
Foliage:	Small, neat, heart-shaped; later large, bluntly rounded; more or less evergreen.
Size:	Up to 9m (30ft) high, often less; 3–4m (10–13ft) wide.
Positioning:	Light or semi-shade, sheltered from frost and cold winds; in well-drained garden soil (not chalky) or in a cool conservatory.
Care:	Plant in spring in well-dug soil with added bonemeal. Water in a dry season. Feed in spring with general fertilizer, mulch with compost. Stems are self-supporting.
Propagation:	Grow cuttings under glass in spring; layer in autumn.
Recommended:	Basic species and less vigorous 'Minima', variegated 'Sonny', 'Variegata'.
Useful tip:	The common fruiting fig, *F. carica*, is an excellent wall shrub or small tree trained on a warm wall.

Habit: Hardy perennial wall shrub; slender woody stems, upright at first and then arching.

Flowering time: Early and mid-spring.

Foliage: Oval or divided in 3 segments; fresh green; deciduous.

Size: 3m (10ft) or more high, 1.8m (6ft) wide.

Positioning: Full sun or shade, on a tree stump, fence, wall; in rich moist soil.

Care: Plant in autumn or spring in well-dug soil with added compost and bonemeal. Feed after flowering, then mulch. Tie stems to wires. After flowering shorten leading stems by half and flowered side shoots to 5cm (2in) long.

Propagation: Grow cuttings under glass in summer or in a frame in autumn and winter.

Recommended: Dark stemmed *atrocaulis*, large-flowered 'Decipiens'; weeping var. *sieboldii*; cream 'Variegata'.

Useful tip: Neglected plants can be pruned hard after blooms fade, but may then miss a season's flowering.

FORSYTHIA SUSPENSA

This species has a more rambling habit than the forsythia usually grown as a free-standing shrub – one of several × *intermedia* hybrids – and is perfectly suited to cultivation on shady walls. Regular pruning and training creates a framework of branches which are covered with golden blossom early in spring.

Garrya elliptica Tassel Bush

GARRYA ELLIPTICA

Grow this North American shrub, with its long-lasting silvery male catkins that drip profusely from every branch, as a winter highlight. For the rest of the year, use it as a host for summer scramblers like perennial sweet peas or a large-flowered clematis as these will relieve its rather dull foliage.

Habit: Hardy perennial wall shrub or small tree; strong vigorous woody stems.

Flowering time: Late autumn to early spring.

Foliage: Gleaming, dark green or grey-green; wavy-edged; evergreen.

Size: 4m (13ft) high; 3–4m (10–13ft) wide.

Positioning: Full sun or semi-shade, sheltered from strong winter winds, against a large warm wall; in light well-drained soil. Withstands pollution and sea winds.

Care: Plant in early autumn or spring in deeply dug soil with added grit (if heavy) and a little bonemeal. Support is rarely necessary once plants are established. Trim to an upright shape after flowering.

Propagation: Grow cuttings under glass in summer or in a frame in autumn.

Recommended: Basic species, male or female forms, and 'James Roof' with very long male catkins.

Useful tip: Remove one-third of the oldest branches to limit the size of mature specimens.

Hedera algeriensis
Algerian Ivy, Canary Isle Ivy

Habit: Hardy or slightly tender perennial climber; vigorous self-clinging woody stems.

Flowering time: Early autumn onwards.

Foliage: Large, triangular or oval, glossy; bright green or variegated; evergreen.

Size: Up to 6m (20ft) high; 5m (16ft) wide.

Positioning: Sun or shade, sheltered from winds and early morning sunshine, on high walls and fences; in any well-drained soil (not acid).

Care: Plant in autumn or spring in deeply dug soil with added compost or leaf mould. Mulch in autumn. Train early growth towards supports. Trim excess growth in late spring and late summer.

Propagation: Grow cuttings in a frame in summer; layer in autumn.

Recommended: Basic species and 'Ravensholst' (larger leaves), 'Gloire de Marengo' (variegated).

Useful tip: For rapid coverage, lay stems on the soil to root and produce climbing side-shoots.

HEDERA ALGERIENSIS 'GLOIRE DE MARENGO'

This is one of the loveliest ivies, and established plants are an attractive background for perennial flowers. The least hardy, unless grown on a warm wall, it is nonetheless an easy ivy to grow. (syn. *H. canariensis*)

41

Hedera helix Common Ivy

HEDERA HELIX

Common ivy is an extremely variable plant and has produced dozens of exciting varieties, from miniatures for clothing low retaining walls or tree stumps, to strong hearty climbers that could cover a house. All are decorative and popular, not just with gardeners but also with wildlife.

Habit: Hardy perennial climber; vigorous self-clinging woody stems.

Flowering time: From early autumn, at top of supports.

Foliage: Shapes vary, often changing on flowering shoots; green or variegated; evergreen.

Size: 5–6m (16–20ft) or more high; 5m (16ft) wide.

Positioning: Full sun or light shade (deep shade for green forms), on sound walls fences, free-standing supports; in well-drained soil (not acid).

Care: Plant in autumn or spring in deeply dug soil with added compost or leaf mould. Train to supports and tie in until aerial rooting starts. Trim in spring, late summer.

Propagation: Grow cuttings in a frame in summer; layer in autumn.

Recommended: 'Harrison', 'Pedata' (especially hardy); 'Emerald Globe', 'Glacier' (for low walls); 'Cathedral Wall' (most vigorous).

Useful tip: Some varieties take a year or more to start climbing in earnest.

Holboellia coriacea
Holboellia

Habit: Hardy perennial climber; fast-growing slender twining stems.

Flowering time: Mid- and late spring.

Foliage: Divided into 3 oval or lance-shaped leaflets; dark green, leathery; evergreen.

Size: 6–7m (20–23ft) high; up to 3m (10ft) wide.

Positioning: Full sun (semi-shade tolerated), sheltered from cold winds, on a warm wall or pergola; in any fertile soil.

Care: Plant in autumn or spring in deeply dug soil with added well-rotted manure or compost and bonemeal, and feed with general fertilizer. Mulch in autumn. Support with wires or trellis or allow to scramble into a tree. No pruning is required.

Propagation: Grow cuttings under glass in spring or summer.

Recommended: Basic species only; also *H. latifolia*, slightly tender with extremely fragrant flowers.

Useful tip: Full sun is essential for a good crop of flowers and fruit.

HOLBOELLIA CORIACEA

This robust Chinese climber is grown as a foliage plant, usually with a companion such as a mid-season or late-flowering clematis to supply later colour. The unisexual blooms are pretty and sweetly fragrant, and followed in a hot season by 5cm (2in) purple fruits.

Humulus lupulus Common Hop

HUMULUS LUPULUS 'AUREUS'

This decorative climber looks stunning scrambling through a large tree or festooned on ropes slung between two poles or walls, especially in autumn when the familiar papery female flowers hang in fat clusters. Hops can be rampant unless trained on ample supports.

Habit: Hardy perennial climber; twining stems.

Flowering time: Late summer to mid-autumn.

Foliage: Rough, toothed, in 3–5 lobes; green or gold; deciduous.

Size: 6m (20ft) or more high; up to 3m (10ft) wide.

Positioning: Full sun (for gold form) or semi-shade, with shelter from winds, on a pergola, trellis or wires; rich moist soil.

Care: Plant in spring in deeply dug soil with plenty of compost or leaf mould and feed with general fertilizer. Mulch in autumn with well-rotted manure. Water in dry weather. Thin young shoots to 5–6 per crown, and train towards wires or strings. Cut growth to ground in late autumn.

Propagation: Grow cuttings under glass in summer; divide in spring.

Recommended: Basic species and golden 'Aureus'; also *H. japonicus* and 'Variegatus'.

Useful tip: Gather green female 'cones' in autumn and hang them up to dry.

Ipomoea lobata Spanish Flag

Habit: Slightly tender perennial climber (often grown as an annual); vigorous red twining woody stems.

Flowering time: Mid-summer to mid-autumn.

Foliage: Coarsely toothed, ivy-shaped or divided into 3 lobes; bright green; deciduous or semi-evergreen.

Size: 3m (10ft) high; 1.5m (5ft) wide.

Positioning: Full sun, sheltered from winds and frost, on canes or wires; in rich moist soil.

Care: Plant after spring frosts in well-dug soil with plenty of compost and feed with general fertilizer; water when dry. Train stems on canes or wires, or let them scramble into shrubs. Protect roots with straw or bracken over winter.

Propagation: Grow cuttings under glass in summer.

Recommended: Basic species only; also *I. indica* in a frost free conservatory.

Useful tip: Grow outdoors in large pots and overwinter under frost-free glass.

IPOMOEA LOBATA

The bright leaves of this colourful perennial, with their distinctive long central lobes and red stalks, are pleasing but it is the ever-changing blooms that attract most attention as they mature from crimson to yellow and then finally white. (syns *Mina lobata*, *Quamoclit lobata*.)

Ipomoea tricolor Morning Glory

IPOMOEA TRICOLOR 'HEAVENLY BLUE'

Watching the long pointed flower buds unfurl in the early morning sunshine is one of summer's great joys; each 10cm (4in) silky bloom fades before the end of the day, but others follow in a continuous sequence. (syns *I. rubro-coerulea*, *Pharbitis tricolor*.)

Habit:	Tender perennial climber (usually grown as an annual); slender twining stems.
Flowering time:	Mid-summer until autumn frosts.
Foliage:	Soft, heart-shaped; bright green; deciduous.
Size:	3–4m (10–13ft) high; 90cm–1.2m (3–4ft) wide.
Positioning:	Full sun, sheltered from winds, on canes, wires or trained up a host plant; in rich moist soil.
Care:	Plant pot-grown plants after last frosts in well-dug soil with plenty of compost. Feed now and then with general fertilizer; water when dry. Deadhead if flowering dwindles.
Propagation:	Sow seeds soaked in tepid water for 12 hours under glass in mid-spring; transplant to small pots.
Recommended:	'Heavenly Blue' and 'Pearly Gates' (syn. 'White Magic').
Useful tip:	On dry soils mulch after planting and site well away from host; steer plants to supports with canes.

Jasminum nudiflorum Winter Jasmine

Habit: Hardy perennial wall shrub; long arching green stems.

Flowering time: Mid-autumn to early spring.

Foliage: Small, oval; shiny, dark green; deciduous.

Size: Up to 3m (10ft) high; 3m (10ft) wide.

Positioning: Full sun or semi-shade, on a fence, wall, pillar; in any soil.

Care: Plant in autumn or spring in soil with forked-in bonemeal or general fertilizer. Feed in spring or mulch with compost. Train stems on wires or trellis, and let them arch from the top. Trim to size with shears after flowering; on mature plants remove one-third of older stems, shorten younger shoots where necessary.

Propagation: Grow cuttings under glass in summer or in a frame in autumn.

Recommended: Basic species and variegated 'Aureum' and 'Mystique'.

Useful tip: To produce a weeping tree, train several stems up a free-standing pillar and let them cascade down.

JASMINUM NUDIFLORUM

The evergreen stems of winter jasmine are studded with soft yellow blooms that resemble primroses. Sudden frosts may spoil open flowers at times during winter, but just a few days of sunshine are enough to coax the next flush of buds to open. Plants always flower more profusely against a sunny wall.

Jasminum officinale Common Jasmine

Habit: Hardy perennial climber; very vigorous twining woody stems.

Flowering time: Early summer to early autumn.

Foliage: Divided into 5–9 leaflets; dark green, slightly downy; more or less evergreen.

Size: Up to 10m (33ft) high; 3m (10ft) wide.

Positioning: Full sun (for flowers) or very light shade, on a strong support; in any fairly fertile soil.

Care: Plant in autumn or spring in well-dug soil with added compost and bonemeal. Feed in spring with general fertilizer, mulch light soils. Fan out stems initially on wires or trellis. Thin out tangled stems after flowering to keep growth within bounds.

Propagation: Grow cuttings in a frame in summer.

Recommended: Basic species, larger flowered *affine* (syn. 'Grandiflorum'), 'Argenteovariegatum', (variegated), 'Aureum'; also *J.* × *stephanense*.

Useful tip: Golden 'Aureum' is most dramatic on an evergreen hedge.

JASMINUM OFFICINALE

There are several true climbing jasmines, all easily grown and trained. This is perhaps the most popular – justifiably, because it is a robust fragrant species that withstands urban pollution and thrives in most soils. It is perfect for an arbour or pergola.

Lapageria rosea Chilean Bellflower

Habit: Slightly tender perennial climber; twining woody stems.

Flowering time: Early summer to mid-autumn.

Foliage: Oblong, tough and leathery; dark green; evergreen.

Size: Up to 5m (16ft) high; 1.2m (4ft) wide.

Positioning: Light shade, on a warm sheltered wall or under glass; in moist leafy, slightly acid soil.

Care: Plant in spring in deeply dug soil with plenty of compost or leaf mould and a little bonemeal and feed with general fertilizer. Water occasionally in a dry season. Train on wires or trellis. Prune to shape if necessary after flowering.

Propagation: Sow seeds under glass in spring; layer in spring or autumn.

Recommended: Basic species, 'Flesh Pink' and 'Nash Court' (both pink), and var. *albiflora* and 'White Cloud' (both white).

Useful tip: Slugs are particularly fond of young growth, so protect new shoots in the early stages.

LAPAGERIA ROSEA

This glorious climber revels in the shelter of a cool conservatory or porch, where its blooms can be seen centre-stage. They grow up to 10cm (4in) long, and are so firm and waxy that they squeak when handled. Plants are also hardy in mild sheltered gardens, or may be grown in large containers of lime-free compost enriched with a little manure.

Lathyrus latifolius Perennial Sweet Pea

LATHYRUS LATIFOLIUS

This old cottage garden perennial is usually seen rambling over shrubs and hedges, where its dense clusters of shapely blooms are shown off more effectively than if it were trained against a wall. Established plants often seed freely but seedlings must be moved while still very young. Flowers are ideal for cutting.

Habit: Hardy perennial climber; winged stems and tendrils.

Flowering time: Mid-summer to early autumn.

Foliage: Divided into several leaflets and ending in pairs of tendrils; crisp and mid-green.

Size: Up to 3m (10ft) high; 1.2–1.5m (4–5ft) wide.

Positioning: Full sun or very light shade, beside a strong host shrub, on trellis; in any fertile soil.

Care: Plant in autumn or spring in deeply dug soil with plenty of compost or well-rotted manure. Dress with bonemeal in spring; feed with general fertilizer at mid-summer. Water occasionally in dry weather. Train initially on to supports. Cut top growth to ground level in late autumn.

Propagation: Divide roots in spring; sow seeds in a frame in spring.

Recommended: Basic species and 'Albus', 'Pink Pearl', 'Red Pearl'.

Useful tip: Divided roots take 1–2 seasons to establish.

Lathyrus odoratus Sweet Pea

Habit: Hardy annual climber; slightly downy stems and leaf tendrils.

Flowering time: Early summer to early autumn.

Foliage: Brittle and divided into pairs of leaflets with tendrils; light or mid-green; deciduous.

Size: Up to 1.8m (6ft) high; 30cm (12in) wide.

Positioning: Full sun, best as a screen on netting, canes or trellis panels; in rich moist soil.

Care: Grow in spring 15–23cm (6–9in) apart in deeply dug soil with plenty of well-rotted manure, a little lime. Mulch to keep roots cool and moist; feed fortnightly with general fertilizer after flowering starts. Cut or deadhead blooms.

Propagation: Sow seeds in small pots under glass in mid- or late autumn, plant out in mid-spring Sow in situ in spring.

Recommended: Galaxy, Spencer and Royal strains; many good varieties.

Useful tip: Seeds of some forms must be nicked or pre-soaked overnight in order to germinate.

LATHYRUS ODORATUS 'KIRI TE KANAWA'

Annual sweet peas need no introduction, for they are everyone's favourite climber – as garden decoration and also for supplying armfuls of long-stemmed cut flowers. Choose varieties carefully if you want the best scent, because breeding has often emphasized colour and size at the expense of fragrance.

Lonicera japonica Japanese Honeysuckle

LONICERA JAPONICA 'HALLIANA'

This oriental species is deservedly popular for its long continuous season of fragrant blooms that sparkle in the sunlight among its evergreen or semi-evergreen foliage, making a charming pattern of green, white and yellow. Growth is vigorous, but plants withstand hard pruning.

Habit: Hardy perennial climber; vigorous woody twining stems.

Flowering time: Early summer to mid-autumn.

Foliage: Softly hairy, oval or lobed; bright green; more or less evergreen.

Size: Up to 9m (30ft) high; 1.8m (6ft) wide.

Positioning: Full sun with roots in shade, trained on a pergola, hedge or tree; in rich moist soil.

Care: Plant in autumn or spring in deeply dug soil with plenty of compost or well-rotted manure. Mulch in spring with manure or feed with high-potash fertilizer. Water now and then in dry weather. Train young stems on canes or wires. Prune in early spring to limit spread.

Propagation: Grow cuttings under glass in summer or layer in autumn.

Recommended: Basic species, 'Hall's Prolific', 'Halliana', 'Aureoreticulata' (gold-veined) and var. *repens* (purple-tinted).

Useful tip: Watch out for aphids in summer.

Lonicera periclymenum
Common Honeysuckle, Woodbine

Habit:	Hardy perennial climber; moderately vigorous twining woody stems.
Flowering time:	Early summer to early autumn.
Foliage:	Oval or oblong; rich green; deciduous.
Size:	Up to 4m (13ft) high; 1.2m (4ft) wide.
Positioning:	Light shade with tops in sunlight, trained informally on shrubs, hedges; in fairly fertile well-drained soil.
Care:	Plant in autumn or spring in deeply dug soil with plenty of compost or leaf mould. Feed in spring with general fertilizer or mulch with compost. Tie in young growth to scramble over a host plant. After flowering, thin growth and cut weak shoots almost to their base.
Propagation:	Grow cuttings under glass in summer, in a frame in late autumn.
Recommended:	'Belgica' (Early Dutch), 'Graham Thomas', 'Serotina' (Late Dutch), variegated 'Harlequin'.
Useful tip:	Combine 'Belgica' and 'Serotina' for the best sequence of bloom.

LONICERA PERICLYMENUM 'BELGICA'

This is the old-fashioned wild woodbine of country hedgerows and cottage gardens. Choice varieties are a little more formal in appearance, but all kinds can be left to roam at will. They produce large and very fragrant blooms all summer which are followed by clusters of red berries.

Lophospermum erubescens Creeping Gloxinia

LOPHOSPERMUM ERUBESCENS

This lovely Mexican vine is the perfect climber for a cool conservatory, but may also be grown in pots, either permanently for standing outdoors on a patio in summer, or for planting out for the season. (syns *Asarina erubescens, Maurandia erubescens*.)

Habit: Tender perennial climber (often grown as an annual); soft twining stems.

Flowering time: Mid-summer to early autumn.

Foliage: Soft, hairy, triangular and toothed; greyish-green; evergreen.

Size: Up to 3m (10ft) high; 90cm (3ft) wide.

Positioning: Full sun or very light shade, as an annual in rich moist soil or in a cool conservatory.

Care: Plant after the last frosts in soil lightly forked over with some compost, and mulch. Water when dry. Feed regularly with liquid general fertilizer while flowering. Train on trellis, wires. Trim to shape after flowering.

Propagation: Sow seeds under glass in early spring, grow singly in pots; grow cuttings under glass in summer.

Recommended: Basic species; also *L. scandens*, related varieties of *Asarina* and *Maurandia*.

Useful tip: Dig up and pot outdoor plants in autumn and overwinter under glass.

Habit: Hardy perennial wall shrub or tree; large spreading branches.

Flowering time: Mid-summer to mid-autumn in flushes.

Foliage: Large; glossy and rich green, may be rusty beneath; evergreen.

Size: Up to 12m (40ft) high; 6–9m (20–30ft) wide.

Positioning: Full sun, sheltered from strong winds, against a spacious high wall; in deep rich soil, well-drained and ideally slightly acid.

Care: Plant in spring in deeply dug soil with plenty of compost or well-rotted manure and mulch lavishly with leaf mould, or compost mixed with manure. Tie branches to wall nails or wires. Prune to shape if necessary in spring.

Propagation: Layer in spring.

Recommended: Basic species and 'Ferruginea', 'Goliath', 'Exmouth' (syn. 'Lanceolata'); also *M. sieboldii* and *M. wilsonii* (best in semi-shade).

Useful tip: If leaves turn yellow water with sequestered iron.

MAGNOLIA GRANDIFLORA

This must be the most aristocratic of all the various magnolias, especially when grown against a house wall two storeys or more in height. The bold foliage is a handsome foil for the huge flowers, which are heavily fragrant and up to 30cm (12in) across in the variety 'Goliath'.

Parthenocissus Virginia Creeper

PARTHENOCISSUS HENRYANA

The impact of the vivid autumn leaf colours of these handsome Virginia creepers is breathtaking, especially where plants are trained high into trees or fanned out to cover a whole wall. Most species secure themselves to supports with self-adhesive pads.

Habit:	Hardy perennial climber; woody stems and tendrils.
Flowering time:	Early summer (insignificant).
Foliage:	Large, velvety, divided into 3–5 leaflets; green or bronze, brilliant tints in autumn; deciduous.
Size:	9–15m (30–50ft) high; 6m (20ft) or more wide.
Positioning:	Full sun or semi-shade (for autumn colour), on a large wall or tree; in moist fertile soil.
Care:	Plant in autumn or spring in deeply dug soil with plenty of compost or leaf mould. Mulch in spring and feed young plants with general fertilizer. Secure stems to wall-ties if necessary. To limit growth, trim after leaf-fall, and while growing if necessary.
Propagation:	Grow cuttings in a frame in summer.
Recommended:	*P. quinquefolia;* *P. tricuspidata,* especially 'Veitchii'; *P. henryana.*
Useful tip:	After pruning remove adhesive-pad marks left on walls with a wire brush.

Passiflora caerulea Passion-flower

Habit: Hardy or slightly tender perennial climber; vigorous woody stems and tendrils.

Flowering time: Early summer to early autumn.

Foliage: 5–7 lobes; glossy, dark green; more or less evergreen.

Size: Up to 9m (30ft) high; 6m (20ft) wide.

Positioning: Full sun, sheltered from frost and winds, on a wall; in poorish soil with minimum lime.

Care: Plant in spring in deeply dug soil with a little added leaf mould (ideally restrict root-run with tiles) and feed with high-potash fertilizer. Train stems on wires or trellis. In cold areas cover base and main stems with sacking. In spring thin and shorten stems.

Propagation: Grow cuttings under glass in mid-summer; sow seeds under glass in spring.

Recommended: Basic species and 'Constance Elliott' (ivory white).

Useful tip: For prolific flowering, avoid nitrogen-rich fertilizers and train stems horizontally.

PASSIFLORA CAERULEA

In most gardens this is the best passion-flower to grow outdoors. Even when cut to the ground by an exceptionally hard frost, it will usually revive in the following spring to give a fine display of its flowers, followed in autumn by orange fruits the size of bantam eggs.

Pileostegia viburnoides Pileostegia

PILEOSTEGIA VIBURNOIDES

This Himalayan species was introduced only this century and is already proving itself to be one of the best evergreen climbers for a fully shaded wall. The shiny leaves are handsome, especially when backing the dense frothy clusters of tiny white flowers with conspicuous stamens. (syn. *Schizophragma viburnoides*.)

Habit: Hardy perennial climber; slow-growing, self-clinging woody stems.

Flowering time: Mid-summer to early autumn.

Foliage: Lance-shaped; dark green, leathery and glossy; evergreen.

Size: 6–9m (20–30ft) high; 3m (10ft) wide.

Positioning: Sun or shade, on a large wall or tree; in rich moist soil.

Care: Plant plants in spring, in deeply dug soil with plenty of compost or leaf mould; work grit into heavy ground to aid drainage. Mulch well in spring on dry soils. Tie stems to wall nails, wires or canes for the first season or two until self-supporting. Prune in spring if necessary.

Propagation: Grow cuttings under glass in summer; sow seeds in a frame in autumn.

Recommended: Basic species only.

Useful tip: Although plants are fairly slow-growing, allow plenty of space to avoid cramping mature specimens.

Piptanthus nepalensis Evergreen Laburnum

Habit: Hardy or slightly tender perennial wall shrub; upright stems.

Flowering time: Late spring and early summer.

Foliage: Divided into 3 large leaflets, dark blue-green; evergreen except in cold winters.

Size: 2–3m (6½–10ft) high; 1.8m (6ft) wide.

Positioning: Full sun sheltered from cold winds, against a warm wall; in fertile well-drained soil without too much lime.

Care: Plant in spring in well-dug soil with a little added compost or leaf mould (and grit on heavy soils) and feed with high-potash fertilizer. Fan out main stems and tie to wires or trellis. Remove some exhausted stems in late winter, shorten the tallest stems by one-third.

Propagation: Grow cuttings under glass in mid-summer or layer in spring.

Recommended: Basic species only; also *P. tomentosus*.

Useful tip: Plants usually live for 6–10 years; propagate replacements in good time.

PIPTANTHUS NEPALENSIS

This is a brilliant spring-flowering shrub from Himalayan scrubs and woods. Formerly known as *Thermopsis*, it is hardy enough for most gardens but liable to shed its evergreen leaves in a very cold winter. The bright yellow flowers resemble those of a laburnum and are borne in upright cones 8cm (3in) long. (syns *P. laburnifolius, P. forrestii*.)

Pittosporum tenuifolium Pittosporum

PITTOSPORUM TENUIFOLIUM

Pittosporum is a superb foliage plant – and the small spring flowers are also an attractive feature that cannot be ignored when they fill the air with their strong honey fragrance. It is a favourite screening and hedging plant in seaside gardens, but is best grown as a wall shrub elsewhere because of its marginal sensitivity to frost.

Habit: Hardy or slightly tender perennial wall shrub or tree; flexible purple stems.

Flowering time: Mid-spring.

Foliage: Oval with wavy edges; Leathery, glossy; evergreen.

Size: 6m (20ft) or more high; 3m (10ft) wide.

Positioning: Full sun or very light shade, sheltered from cold winds, against a warm wall; in fertile well-drained soil.

Care: Plant in early autumn or late spring in soil with a little compost or leaf mould forked in lightly; add plenty of grit to heavy soils. Water in a dry season. Trim lightly a year after planting for bushy growth; clip to shape in late spring, cut out any winter damage.

Propagation: Grow cuttings under glass in summer.

Recommended: Basic species and variegated 'Eila Keightley' (syn. 'Sunburst'), 'Garnettii', 'Silver Queen'; also drought-resistant *P. tobira*.

Useful tip: Plant *P. dallii* in cold gardens.

Pyracantha Firethorn

Habit:	Hardy perennial wall shrub; vigorous thorny woody stems.
Flowering time:	Late spring and early summer.
Foliage:	Small, oval; dark green and glossy; evergreen.
Size:	3–4.5m (10–15ft) high; 3m (10ft) wide.
Positioning:	Full sun (for berries) or semi-shade, against a wall or fence; in any fertile well-drained soil.
Care:	Plant in autumn or spring in well-dug soil with added compost and bonemeal or general fertilizer, and trim for bushy growth. Mulch in spring, water when dry for the first 2–3 seasons. Tie stems to wires or trellis. Trim to shape in spring, also in summer for formal climbers.
Propagation:	Grow cuttings in a frame in summer.
Recommended:	Variegated 'Harlequin', 'Mohave', 'Navajo', 'Orange Glow', 'Red Column'.
Useful tip:	For rapid coverage, train branches of young plants horizontally, and allow several upright shoots to develop from these.

PYRACANTHA ROGERSIANA

Upright varieties of Pyracantha are designer plants for walls and fences, with easily manipulated branches. Shapes such as espaliers and fans require pruning twice each season, but the extra attention is repaid with a more lavish display of berries in autumn.

61

Rhodochiton atrosanguineus Purple Bellerine

RHODOCHITON ATROSANGUINEUS

The 5cm (2in) purple blooms on this opulent climber from Mexico appear in masses all season, and their conspicuous reddish-pink inflated calyces linger long after the petals have fallen. (syn. *R. volubile*.)

Habit:	Tender perennial climber (often grown as an annual); slender stems and twining leaf stalks.
Flowering time:	Late spring to mid-autumn.
Foliage:	Toothed, heart-shaped or lobed; evergreen above 7°C (45°F).
Size:	3–5m (10–16ft) high; 1.2m (4ft) wide.
Positioning:	Light or dappled shade, in sheltered warmth; in well-drained leafy soil or under cool glass.
Care:	Plant after the last frosts in well-dug soil with plenty of compost or leaf mould (and grit if drainage is suspect), feed with general fertilizer and mulch. In autumn protect roots with straw or leaves. Train stems on trellis, wires or canes. Thin out and shorten shoots in late winter.
Propagation:	Grow cuttings under glass in summer; sow under glass in spring.
Recommended:	Basic species only.
Useful tip:	Train 3 plants on a tripod of canes in a pot; treat as annuals.

Rosa 'Buff Beauty' Shrub Rose

Habit:	Hardy perennial hybrid musk rose; vigorous thorny arching stems.
Flowering time:	Mid-summer to early autumn, in flushes.
Foliage:	Dark green with a purple tint; deciduous.
Size:	2.4m (8ft) or more high on a wall; 1.5m (5ft) wide.
Positioning:	Full sun or dappled shade, on a fence or wall; in deep rich soil.
Care:	Plant firmly in autumn in deeply dug soil with plenty of well-rotted manure or compost and bonemeal. Mulch in spring. Feed with rose fertilizer once or twice in summer. Shape plants in early spring to encourage strong upright stems; tie these to wires or wall nails. Deadhead to strong side-shoots.
Propagation:	Grow 30cm (12in) cuttings outdoors in autumn.
Recommended:	'Abraham Darby', 'Cornelia', 'Fountain', 'Jacqueline du Pré', 'Leander', 'Nevada', 'Nymphenburg'.
Useful tip:	Water plants at the dry base of a brick or stone wall regularly.

ROSA 'BUFF BEAUTY'

Many shrub roses produce long, upright or arching stems that can be fanned out and trained against a wall or fence, or may be gathered together on a pillar. In these situations some kinds can double their normal height: 'Buff Beauty' is typical, its slightly awkward arching stems adapting perfectly to wall-training.

Rosa 'Compassion' Climbing Rose

ROSA 'COMPASSION'

Habit: Hardy perennial climber; robust permanent stems from the base.

Flowering time: Summer and autumn.

Foliage: Large, deep green; healthy; deciduous.

Size: 3m (10ft) high, 3m (10ft) wide.

Positioning: Full sun or very light shade, on a pillar, tripod, fence or white wall; in deep rich soil.

Care: Plant firmly in autumn in deeply dug soil with plenty of well-rotted manure. Mulch in spring. Feed with rose fertilizer once or twice in summer. For the first 2 seasons tie in stems to wires or wall nails to establish a framework; then prune in early spring: cut out dead and old stems, shorten long side-shoots by two-thirds.

Propagation: May be grown from 30cm (12in) cuttings outdoors in autumn.

Recommended: 'Alister Stella Gray', 'Gloire de Dijon', 'Schoolgirl', thornless 'Zéphirine Drouhin'.

Useful tip: Shorten long stems in late autumn to avoid wind damage.

It is almost impossible to overrate the finest varieties of climbing roses, which provide such a beautiful and dependable display of colour on walls. Some are very old, others (such as 'Compassion') up-to-date, but all climbers have fairly stiff stems that develop into a permanent framework.

Rosa 'Rambling Rector' Rambler Rose

Habit: Hardy perennial rambler; long flexible branching stems.

Flowering time: Mid-summer.

Foliage: Small and prolific, healthy; grey-green; deciduous.

Size: 6m (20ft) or more high; up to 4.5m (15ft) wide.

Positioning: Sun or shade, on a large sturdy structure; in deep fertile soil.

Care: Plant firmly in autumn in well-dug soil with plenty of decayed manure or compost and bonemeal. Mulch in spring. Feed with bonemeal in autumn. Train stems on canes into tree branches or on horizontal wires. Prune if space is limited: replace some older branches with young stems after flowering.

Propagation: Grow 30cm (12in) cuttings outdoors in autumn.

Recommended: 'Albertine', 'Crimson Shower', 'Félicité Perpétue', 'New Dawn', 'Seagull'.

Useful tip: Plant in woodland and hedges to ramble freely.

ROSA 'RAMBLING RECTOR'

Some ramblers are compact and restrained, whereas others such as 'Rambling Rector' are on a huge scale with masses of leaves, flowers and fragrance. Most are almost like wild plants, and pruning is usually optional.

Rubus Bramble

RUBUS 'OREGON THORNLESS'

The bramble family is huge and variable, and includes several very hardy and non-aggressive forms which are both decorative and productive. For training in a prominent position, always choose varieties with special features such as variegated foliage, attractive berries or thornless stems.

Habit:	Hardy perennial wall shrub; long rambling stems may be prickly.
Flowering time:	Early to mid-summer.
Foliage:	Maple-shaped or deeply cut; dark green or variegated, rich autumn tints; ever-green or deciduous.
Size:	1.8–3m (6–10ft) high; 1.8–3m (6–10ft) wide.
Positioning:	Sun or shade, on a wall, fence or pergola, on wires as a screen; in rich moist soil.
Care:	Plant in autumn or spring in deeply dug soil with plenty of well-rotted manure or compost and cut down to 23cm (9in). Mulch in spring with manure. Water now and then in dry weather. Train stems evenly on parallel wires or trellis. After fruiting replace exhausted stems with young canes.
Propagation:	Layer tips of stems in autumn.
Recommended:	*R. fruticosus* (Blackberry); *R. phoenicolasius* (Japanese Wineberry).
Useful tip:	Poor soils can enhance autumn tints but depress fruiting.

Schisandra rubriflora Schisandra

Habit: Hardy or slightly tender perennial climber; twining woody stems.

Flowering time: Mid-spring to early summer.

Foliage: Leathery and toothed; lance-shaped; bright green; deciduous.

Size: Up to 6m (20ft) high; 3m (10ft) wide.

Positioning: Dappled sunlight or semi-shade, on a wall, fence or ornamental structure; in moist fertile soil.

Care: Plant in autumn or spring in deeply dug soil with plenty of compost, or leaf mould and bonemeal. Feed in spring with general fertilizer, mulch lavishly on hot dry soils. Train stems on wires or trellis. In winter cut out some of the oldest stems and shorten any that are too long.

Propagation: Grow cuttings in a frame in summer; layer in autumn.

Recommended: Basic species only; also S. grandiflora, (pink or white); S. propinqua var. chinensis (orange).

Useful tip: Keep roots cool and moist at all times.

SCHISANDRA RUBRIFLORA

Male and female plants are equally attractive in flower, but both are needed if the females are to develop their spectacular 10cm (4in) spikes of bright red fruits. Grow where you can sit and enjoy the spicy fragrance of the blooms.

Schizophragma hydrangeoides Schizophragma

SCHIZOPHRAGMA HYDRANGEOIDES

This shrub has a 'lacecap' flowerhead arrangement of tiny fertile blooms gathered in central florets and surrounded by larger outer petals which are long-lasting, and papery in texture.

Habit:	Hardy perennial wall shrub; creeping woody stems and aerial roots.
Flowering time:	Mid-summer to early autumn.
Foliage:	Large, oval and toothed; deep green; deciduous.
Size:	10–12m (33–40ft) high; up to 5m (16ft) wide.
Positioning:	Sun or shade, on high walls, fences, trees; in rich moist soil.
Care:	Plant in autumn or spring in deeply dug soil with plenty of compost or leaf mould. Mulch heavily in spring. Water young plants regularly in dry weather. Tie in stems to wall nails or wires for the first few seasons until plants are self-supporting. Pruning is rarely necessary but may be done in spring.
Propagation:	Grow cuttings under glass in summer.
Recommended:	Basic species and 'Roseum' (pink flowers); also *S. integrifolium* (larger leaves, blooms).
Useful tip:	Plants may need 3–4 seasons before they start to climb.

Solanum crispum Climbing Solanum

Habit: Hardy or slightly tender perennial wall shrub; scrambling woody stems.

Flowering time: Mid-summer to early autumn.

Foliage: Oval or lance-shaped; bright green; more or less evergreen.

Size: 4–6m (13–20ft) high; 1.8m (6ft) wide.

Positioning: Full sun or very light shade, sheltered from cold winds, on shrubs or a warm wall; in any well-drained fertile soil.

Care: Plant in spring in well-dug soil with added compost, or leaf mould and bonemeal, and feed with general fertilizer. Mulch in autumn. Tie to wires or trellis or let stems scramble over tall shrubs. In spring cut back misplaced and weak shoots, remove some old wood.

Propagation: Grow cuttings in a frame in summer.

Recommended: Basic species and 'Glasnevin' (syn. 'Autumnale').

Useful tip: Protect stems with sacking or fleece if temperatures drop below −5°C (23°F).

SOLANUM CRISPUM 'GLASNEVIN'

One of the loveliest members of the nightshade family, this Chilean species may be grown as a free-standing shrub in the open in mild gardens, but usually prefers the shelter of a warm wall, where its flowers appear as a billowing mass of purple and bright yellow.

Stauntonia hexaphylla  Stauntonia

STAUNTONIA HEXAPHYLLA

This Japanese climber is very vigorous and will rapidly cover a warm wall or sheltered pergola. The fragrant blooms resemble pale violet snowdrops, and are produced on male and female plants alike – both are needed to produce the edible purple 5cm (2in) fruits.

Habit: Hardy or slightly tender perennial climber; slender twining woody stems.

Flowering time: Mid- and late spring.

Foliage: Divided into 3–7 oval leaflets; leathery, dark green; more or less evergreen.

Size: Up to 9m (30ft) high; 3m (10ft) wide.

Positioning: Full sun or semi-shade, on a warm sheltered wall or fence; in light fertile soil with minimum lime.

Care: Plant in spring in deeply dug soil with plenty of compost or leaf mould and feed with general fertilizer. Mulch in autumn. Let stems ramble in tall shrubs, or tie to trellis or wires. Shorten long shoots as necessary in late winter.

Propagation: Grow cuttings under glass in spring or layer in summer.

Recommended: Basic species only; also *S. latifolia* (see *Holboellia latifolia*).

Useful tip: Mulched plants that have been cut down by a hard frost revive from ground level.

Thunbergia alata Black-eyed Susan

Habit: Tender perennial climber (usually grown as an annual); slender twining stems.

Flowering time: Early summer to early autumn.

Foliage: Large; toothed, heart-shaped; deciduous.

Size: Up to 3m (10ft) high; 45–60cm (18–24in) wide.

Positioning: Full sun, on trellis or wires, under cool glass or outdoors in a sheltered site in well-drained fertile soil.

Care: Plant after the last frosts in well-dug soil with added compost or leaf mould (add grit to heavy soils); mulch. Water in dry weather. Feed once or twice while in flower. Train on supports. In late winter prune to shape. Protect from frost.

Propagation: Grow cuttings under glass in summer; sow seeds under glass in early spring, transplant individually to pots.

Recommended: Basic species and 'Susie Mixed'; also *T. fragrans*.

Useful tip: If grown as an annual, trail 3 plants from a hanging basket.

THUNBERGIA ALATA

Thunbergias are usually grown as annuals but will survive if kept above freezing point and produce stronger growth and earlier flowers in succeeding years. For the best results grow in a greenhouse or conservatory border, or in pots outdoors for housing under glass in autumn.

Trachelospermum jasminoides Chinese Jasmine

TRACHELOSPERMUM JASMINOIDES

The fragrant blooms of this beautiful self-supporting climber have been compared variously to jasmine and periwinkle, and appear in large numbers on established plants. Chinese jasmine enjoys growing in coastal gardens, where it copes easily with salt spray, but inland it needs warm shelter or conservatory conditions.

Habit: Hardy or slightly tender perennial climber; slow-growing twining woody stems.

Flowering time: Mid- and late summer.

Foliage: Oval, glossy, leathery; dark green (often turning crimson in winter); more or less evergreen.

Size: 6–7.5m (20–25ft) high; 6m (20ft) wide.

Positioning: Full sun, on a warm sheltered wall; in any fertile soil without excessive lime.

Care: Plant in spring in deeply dug soil with plenty of compost or leaf mould (add grit to heavy soils) and feed with general fertilizer. Protect roots in autumn with straw or leaves. Train on wires or trellis. In spring cut out winter damage and trim to shape.

Propagation: Grow cuttings under glass in late summer or layer in spring.

Recommended: Basic species and 'Japonicum', 'Wilsonii' and 'Variegatum'.

Useful tip: *T. asiaticum* is hardier where temperatures fall much below −5°C (23°F).

Habit:	Hardy or tender annual climber; vigorous rambling stems.
Flowering time:	Early summer to early autumn.
Foliage:	Large, shield-shaped; bright green or variegated; deciduous.
Size:	1.8–2.4m (6–8ft) high; 1.8m (6ft) wide.
Positioning:	Full sun or very light shade, against walls, fences, hedges, shrubs; in well-drained soil with low fertility.
Care:	Plant or sow in late spring, 20cm (8in) apart, in lightly forked soil with a little added compost. Water regularly in a dry season and mulch with grass clippings on very light soils. Let stems ramble freely, or tuck behind wires or trellis. Watch out for aphids and caterpillars.
Propagation:	Sow seeds indoors in late winter, or in situ in spring.
Recommended:	Mixtures of tall hybrids and named varieties like 'Climbing Jewel of Africa' (variegated).
Useful tip:	Grow in herb gardens: flowers, leaves and seeds are all edible.

TROPAEOLUM MAJUS

Tall nasturtium varieties produce bright yellow, orange and red flowers shaped like trumpets and bold peppery tasting leaves in great quantities. This ensures their popularity as fast-growing climbers for new gardens and wherever gaps appear in more permanent displays. Once grown, there will always be volunteer seedlings for transplanting.

Tropaeolum peregrinum Canary Creeper

TROPAEOLUM PEREGRINUM

This popular climber looks slightly comical when its extravagantly fringed blooms peep from the deeply cut five-fingered leaves. A versatile species, it climbs by means of its leaf stalks and is perfectly adapted to scrambling through tall branching hosts such as climbing roses, clematis and hedging plants.

Habit: Tender annual or short-lived perennial climber; herbaceous stems.

Flowering time: Early summer to mid-autumn.

Foliage: Soft, deeply divided into 5 lobes; light green; deciduous.

Size: Up to 2.5m (8ft) high; 1.2m (4ft) wide.

Positioning: Full sun or very light shade, sheltered from winds, on a warm wall or fence; in well-drained soil with low fertility.

Care: Plant after the last frosts in well-dug soil with added compost. Water regularly in dry weather, and mulch with grass clippings on light soils. Support stems with peasticks, trellis or netting. In mild gardens, cut down top growth in autumn, protect roots with straw or leaves.

Propagation: Sow seeds indoors in late winter or in situ in late spring.

Recommended: Basic species only; also *T. polyphyllum* (yellow or orange).

Useful tip: Sow annually below a purple clematis such as 'Etoile Violette'.

Tropaeolum speciosum Flame Flower

Habit: Hardy perennial climber; wiry twining stems.

Flowering time: Mid-summer to early autumn.

Foliage: Small, neat, divided into 5–7 lobes; bright green; deciduous.

Size: Up to 3m (10ft) high; 1.2–1.8m (4–6ft) wide.

Positioning: Dappled sunlight or semi-shade, especially at the roots, on a cool wall or in shrubs; in moist fertile acid soil.

Care: Plant in spring in well-dug soil with plenty of compost or leaf mould, feed with general fertilizer and mulch on light soils. Water regularly in a dry season. Train stems on trellis, netting or through shrubs. Cut down all top growth in late autumn.

Propagation: Divide roots in spring; sow seeds in a frame in spring.

Recommended: Basic species only; also *T. tuberosum* and 'Ken Aslet' (lift tubers in autumn).

Useful tip: Plants are effective growing through a dark conifer like yew.

TROPAEOLUM SPECIOSUM

This startling Chilean climber is very colourful, with its long-spurred vivid scarlet blooms and blue fruits. It can take 2–3 seasons for the rhizomatous roots to settle down, but once established, plants are reliably hardy. They are particularly eye catching on shaded walls, where they revel in cool moist conditions.

75

Tweedia caerulea Tweedia

TWEEDIA CAERULEA

This shrubby Brazilian species produces masses of pink buds which open into strikingly beautiful flowers, clearest sky blue and fading to purple, lilac. It is reliably perennial only in the warmest gardens, but can be easily grown as an annual outdoors or as a perennial pot plant. (syn. *Oxypetalum caeruleum*.)

Habit: Tender perennial climber (often grown as an annual); twining stems.

Flowering time: Mid-summer to early autumn.

Foliage: Large, oval or heart-shaped, silky; grey-green; evergreen above 5°C (41°F).

Size: 90cm (3ft) or more high; 60–90cm (2–3ft) wide.

Positioning: Full sun or very light shade, against a warm wall in summer; in well-drained fertile soil or under cool glass.

Care: Plant after the last frosts in deeply dug soil with added leaf mould (add grit to heavy soils); mulch. Feed once or twice in summer. Pinch out tips of young shoots. Train stems on wires or peasticks. Pot up in autumn and overwinter indoors. Prune to shape in early spring.

Propagation: Grow cuttings under glass in late spring.

Recommended: Basic species only.

Useful tip: Keep plants in pots and stand them outdoors in summer as patio climbers.

Viburnum macrocephalum · Chinese Snowball Tree

Habit: Hardy perennial wall shrub; branching woody stems.

Flowering time: Late spring.

Foliage: Large, thin; matt green; deciduous or semi-evergreen.

Size: Up to 6m (20ft) high; 4m (13ft) or more wide.

Positioning: Full sun or semi-shade, on a sheltered fence or wall; in deep moist soil.

Care: Plant in spring in deeply dug soil with plenty of compost, leaf mould or decayed manure, feed with general fertilizer and mulch on drier soils. Tie in branches to wires or wall nails. Prune to shape after flowering: shorten vigorous branches, cut out misplaced shoots.

Propagation: Grow cuttings under glass in summer or in a frame in autumn.

Recommended: Basic species and selected form 'Sterile'; V. × burkwoodii, especially 'Anne Russell', 'Fulbrook', 'Park Farm Hybrid'.

Useful tip: Avoid extremely wet or dry soils below walls.

VIBURNUM MACROCEPHALUM

All the Viburnums are adaptable plants, but none more so than this. Its growth habit makes it particularly suitable as a wall shrub, the handsome foliage contrasting well with brick or stonework. Combine with V. × burkwoodii for blooms from mid-winter to late spring.

Vitis coignetiae Ornamental Grape Vine

VITIS COIGNETIAE

Ornamental vines are popular and handsome climbers, with varied leaf shapes and sumptuous tints in autumn. Many also bear decorative or edible grapes. This is a typical robust variety for a high wall or pergola, and is capable of reaching the top of a large tree.

Habit: Hardy perennial climber; long flexible stems, strong tendrils.

Flowering time: Late spring and early summer.

Foliage: Large, 3–5 deep lobes; bright green (purple and gold in autumn); deciduous.

Size: Up to 9–12m (30–40ft) high; 9m (30ft) wide.

Positioning: Full sun, sheltered from cold winds, on a wall, pergola or tree; in deep well-drained, not too acid, soil.

Care: Plant in autumn or spring in deeply dug soil with plenty of compost or leaf mould. Train on strong canes into trees or on wires. Leave vines in trees unpruned. Shorten the previous year's shoots on others almost to their base in winter; prune growing tips 2–3 times in summer.

Propagation: Grow cuttings under glass in spring or autumn.

Recommended: *V. coignetiae*; also *V. 'Purpurea'*, *V. 'Brant'*.

Useful tip: Soils with low fertility give the best colours.

Vitis vinifera Grape Vine

Habit: Hardy perennial climber; long flexible stems and tendrils.

Flowering time: Late spring and early summer.

Foliage: Large, palm-shaped, 3–7 lobes; deciduous.

Size: Up to 6m (20ft) high; 5–6m (16–20ft) wide.

Positioning: Full sun, sheltered from winds, on a wall or posts and wires; in deep well-drained soil.

Care: Plant in autumn or spring in deeply dug soil with plenty of bonemeal and compost. Feed in spring with general fertilizer, mulch with well-rotted manure. Cut back stems after planting and train branches on horizontal wires; shorten fruiting side-shoots to 2 buds in winter and remove growing tips 2 leaves beyond a flower truss.

Propagation: Grow cuttings under glass in spring or autumn.

Recommended: 'New York Muscat' (dessert), 'Madeleine Sylvaner', (wine).

Useful tip: Consult a specialist about varieties for particular districts.

VITIS VINIFERA 'BLACK HAMBURG'

Home grown grapes are something to boast about. You will need to wait three years after planting, but outdoor vines will then yield annually for 40 years or more. Although plants need regular attention, the results always justify this.

Wisteria Wisteria

WISTERIA SINENSIS 'ALBA'

One of the best-known climbers and often the first choice for a house wall, wisteria can live for several centuries and produces masses of wonderful blossom every year if pruned carefully. Both the main species are equally beautiful with cones of fragrant blooms 10–90cm (4–36in) in length.

Habit: Hardy perennial climber; twining stems become branches.

Flowering time: Late spring and early summer.

Foliage: Long, divided into 7–19 leaflets; lustrous green; deciduous.

Size: 10m (33ft) or more high; up to 30m (100ft) wide.

Positioning: Full sun or very light shade, sheltered from winds, on a large wall, archway or pergola; in deep fertile soil.

Care: Plant in autumn or spring in deeply dug soil with plenty of well-rotted manure or compost. Mulch or feed in spring for the first few years. Train on canes or wires. Shorten leafy shoots to 5 leaves at mid-summer; side-shoots to 2–3 buds in winter.

Propagation: Grow cuttings under glass in late summer or layer in spring.

Recommended: *W. floribunda*, and 'Rosea'; *W. sinensis* and 'Alba'.

Useful tip: Summer pruning is essential for best flowering and to limit invasive growth.